CHRISTMAS CRACKERS

compiled by
matt wilce

FATHER CHRISTMAS

What is Santa's favourite pizza?

One that's deep pan, crisp and even.

What goes red, white, red, white?

Father Christmas rolling down a hill!

Why does Father Christmas go down the chimney?

Because it soots him.

Why does Santa have three gardens?

So he can "Hoe! Hoe! Hoe!"

What kind of motorbike does Father Christmas ride?

A Holly Davidson!

What does Father Christmas do with fat elves?

He sends them to an 'elf farm!

What do you call Santa's little helpers?

Subordinate clauses!

What do Santa's little helpers learn at school?

The elf-abet!

What did Father Christmas say to the smoker?

Please don't smoke, it's bad for my elf!

What do you get if you cross Father Christmas with a detective?

Santa Clues!

What do you call a man who claps at Christmas ?

Santa-plause!

What does Father Christmas call his money ?

Iced lolly!

Why did Father Christmas take a break?

He needed a Santa pause.

What happened when Santa put on weight?

He had a tight Christmas!

What do you call a smelly Santa?

Farter Christmas

What do the reindeer sing to Father Christmas on his birthday ?
Freeze a jolly good fellow!

What's Father Christmas' favourite James Bond film?
Yule Only Live Twice.

What's white and red and goes up and down and up and down?
Santa Claus in an elevator!

What does Santa clean his sleigh with?
Comet.

Why is Santa so good at karate?
Because he has a black belt!

How much did Father Christmas pay for his sleigh?
Nothing, it was on the house!

Who says "Oh, Oh, Oh!"?
Santa walking backwards!

What nationality is Santa Claus?
North Polish.

How do you know when Santa's in the room?

You can sense his presents.

―――――――――――――――――――

CHRISTMAS CREATURES

What do you call a blind reindeer?

No eye deer.

What do you call a dead one-eyed reindeer?

Still no eye deer.

What do you a deer with no eyes and no legs and no ears

Doesn't matter - he can't hear you

What's furry and minty?

A polo bear.

What never eats at Christmas?

The turkey... its stuffed already!

Why did the turkey join the band?

Because it had the drumsticks!

What are the wettest animals in the world?

Reindeer.

What do cows say on December 25th?

Mooey Christmas!

What do you call a penguin in the Sahara desert?

Lost.

What do you get if you cross Father Christmas with a duck?

A Christmas quacker!

What do you call a cat in the desert?

Sandy Claws!

Who delivers presents to baby sharks at Christmas?

Santa Jaws

How long do a reindeers legs have to be?

Long enough so they can touch the ground!

What do reindeer hang on their Christmas trees?

Horn-aments!

Did Rudolph the Red Nosed Reindeer go to school?

No. He was Elf-taught!

Why did the turkey cross the road?

Because it was the chicken's day off!

How do sheep in Spain say Merry Christmas?

Fleece Navidad!

What do monkeys sing at Christmas?

Jungle Bells, Jungle bells...

Why did Scrooge love all of the reindeer?

Because every buck was dear to him!

Which of Santa's reindeer has bad manners?

Rude-olph!

What do you call a reindeer wearing ear muffs?

Anything you want because he can't hear you!

What do reindeer always say before telling you a joke?

This one will sleigh you!

How does Rudolph know when Christmas is coming?

He looks at his calen-deer!

What's red and white and gives presents to gazelles?

Santa-lope!

What do you get if you cross a bell with a skunk?

Jingle Smells!

What do sheep say at Christmas?

Wool-tide Bleatings!

Why do so many Christmas cracker jokes feature penguins?

Because joke writers can't spell hippopotamus!

A reindeer walked into a pub, strolled up to the bar and ordered a pint of lager.

Completely un-phased, the barman poured out the lager and passed it to the reindeer, who handed over a ten pound note.

As he handed over the change of a few coins, the barman said, "I have to say, you're first reindeer I've seen in here."

The reindeer studied the change very carefully and said.

"Tell you what sunshine, as these prices I'm also the last reindeer you're going to see in here."

What's red and very fast?

Rudolph's nose!

Why don't penguins fly?

Because they're not tall enough to be pilots!

What do fish sing on December 25th?

Christmas Corals!

What kind of insect hates Christmas?

A humbug.

What is the cleanest reindeer called?

Comet.

During the Christmas special of Mastermind one contestant was asked to name two of Santa's reindeers. The contestant gave a sigh, thinking that he had finally been given an easy question, and answered "Rudolph and Olive!"

"We'll accept Rudolph but can you explain Olive?"

The man looked at the host and said, "You know, Olive the other reindeer, used to laugh and call him names..."

What is green, covered with tinsel and goes "ribbet ribbet"?

A mistle-"toad"!

Why is the turkey such a fashionable bird?

Because he's always well dressed when he comes to dinner!

What is white, lives at the north pole and runs around naked?

A polar bare!

How do cats greet each other in December?

Have a furry Merry Christmas and a Happy Mew Year.

How do sheep greet each other in December?

A Merry Christmas to Ewe.

What's Rudolph's favourite day of the year?

Red Nose Day!

Why do reindeer wear fur coats?

Because they would look silly in plastic macs!

Where do you find reindeer?

It depends on where you leave them!

LET IT SNOW!

How do snowmen get around?

They ride an icicle.

———————————

What did one snowman say to the other when the Christmas Number One came on the radio?

That's a cool song!

———————————

What's white and goes up?

A confused snowflake.

———————————

What's worse than Rudolph with a runny nose?

Frosty the snowman with a hot flush!

———————————

What do you get when you cross a snowman with a vampire?

Frostbite!

————

Two snowmen in a field, one turned to the other and said...

"I don't know about you, but I can smell carrots!"

———————————

Two snowmen in a field, one turned to the other and said...

"Can you smell carrots?"

And the second snowman replied, "No, but I can taste coal."

Where would you find chili beans?

At the North Pole!

What do you call a snowman on rollerblades?

A snow mobile.

What falls a lot at Christmas but never gets hurt?

Snow.

What sort of ball doesn't bounce?

A snowball!

What happened when the snowgirl fell out with the snowboy?

She gave him the cold shoulder!

What do snowmen wear on their heads?

Ice caps!

Police were called to a mass grave of dead snow men....

But it turned out to just be a field of carrots!

Where does a snowman keep his money?

In a snow bank.

How do you scare a snowman?

You get a hairdryer!

What do you call a snowman in the summer?

A puddle!

What do you call an old snowman?

Water!

What did Frosty call his cow?

Eskimoo!

What do you call a snowman on roller blades?

A snowmobile!

How do you know when there is a snowman in your bed ?

You wake up wet!

What does Frosty's wife put on her face at night?

Cold cream!

What did Jack Frost say to Frosty the Snowman?

Have an ice day!

What goes: now you see me, now you don't, now you see me, now you don't?

A snowman on a zebra crossing!

What do you sing at a snowman's birthday party?

Freeze a jolly good fellow!

What did Frosty's girlfriend give him when she was mad at him?

The cold shoulder!

Who is Frosty the Snowman's favourite relative?

Aunt Artica!

What does Frosty the Snowman call his dad?

Pop-silcle!

Is it just me, or is unseasonably cold this year?

PRESENTS

What do you give a train driver for Christmas?

Platform shoes.

———————

What do angry mice send each other at Christmas?

Cross-mouse cards.

———————

What did one Christmas tree say to the other?

I've got a present fir you!

———————

What did the dog get for Christmas?

A mobile bone!

———————

What did the farmer get for Christmas?

A cow-culator!

———————

What does Harry Potter use to wrap his presents?

Spell-o-tape!

———————

What did the Christmas tree buy his girlfriend?

A fir coat!

———————

Who delivers Puss in Boots' Christmas presents?

Santa Paws!

Why do Mummies like Christmas so much?

Because of all the wrapping!

I got my mum a wooden leg for Christmas.

It's not her main present, it's just a stocking filler!

"Skywalker, I know what you're getting for Christmas," says Darth Vader.

"How can you possibly know that Vader?" answers Luke.

"I have felt your presents."

What do you get when you cross an archer with giftwrap?

Ribbon Hood.

Dear Father Christmas,
Could you please send me a yellow door.
Yours,
Sherlock Holmes

"So why do you want a yellow door Holmes?" asked Watson.
"Lemon-entry my dear Watson."

What does Mary Poppins want for Christmas?

Superclausfragilisticexpialli-snowshoes!

SEASONAL GUESTS

Knock! Knock!

Who's there?

Snow.

Snow who?

Snow business like show business!

Knock! Knock!

Who's there?

Holly

Holly who?

Holly-days are here again!

Knock! Knock!

Who's there?

Oakham

Oakham who?

Oakham all ye faithful!

Knock! Knock!

Who's there?

Hannah.

Hanna who?

Hannah partridge in a pear tree!

Knock! Knock!

Who's there?

Doughnut

Doughnut who?

Doughnut open until Christmas Day!

Knock! Knock!

Who's there ?

Wayne.

Wayne who ?

Wayne in a manger!

Knock! Knock!

Who's there ?

Avery.

Avery who?

Avery Merry Christmas !

Knock! Knock!

Who's there?

Carol.

Carol who?

Carol singers

━━━━━━━━━━

Knock! Knock!

Who's there?

Police!

Police who?

Police don't make me eat Brussels sprouts this year!

━━━━━━━━━━━━━━━━━━━━

Knock Knock

Who's there?

Wenceslas.

Wenceslas who?

Wenceslas bus home?

━━━━━━━━━━

Knock Knock

Who's there?

Mary.

Mary who?

Mary Christmas!

━━━━━━━━━━

Knock, knock.

Who's there?

Ant

Ant who?

Antartic!

———————

Knock! Knock!

Who's there?

Oh... snowbody's there!

———————

Knock! Knock!

Who's there?

Yule.

Yule who?

Yule never know!

———————

Knock! Knock!

Who's there?

Carol.

Carol who?

Carol Singer!

———————

Knock! Knock!

Who's there?

Snow.

Snow who?

Snow use. I forgot my name again!

===

Knock! Knock!

Who's there?

Irish.

Irish who?

Irish you a Merry Christmas!

===

Knock! Knock!

Who's there?

Abby.

Abby who?

Abby New Year!

===

Knock! Knock!

Who's there?

Lettuce.

Lettuce who?

Lettuce in, it's freezing out here!

===

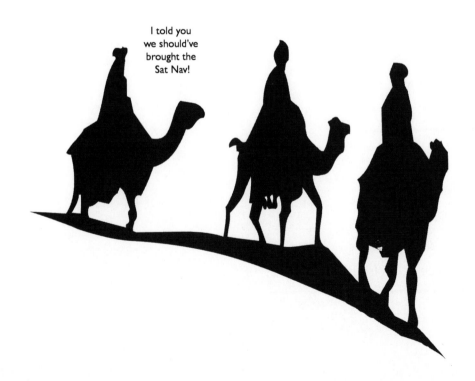

THE CHRISTMAS STORY

Mary said to Joseph, "Put the rubbish out love."
"I can't," he replied.
"It's Christmas – there's no room in the bin."

What carol do they sing in the desert?
Camel All Ye Faithful.

What did Adam say on December 24th?
It's Christmas, Eve.

What comes before Christmas Eve?
Christmas Adam!

What did the Angel Gabriel say to the other angel?
Halo there!

Which football team did the baby Jesus support?
Manger-ster United!

What do crackers, fruitcake and nuts remind me of?

You!

——

CHRISTMAS KITCHEN

Who hides in the bakery at Christmas?

A mince spy.

===

Whats the best thing to put into a Christmas cake ?

Your teeth!

===

What do you get if you cross an apple with a Christmas tree?

A pineapple!

===

What kind of flour do you need for a Christmas pudding?

Elf raising!

===

Why is a Christmas pudding like the ocean?

They are both full of currants.

===

What do you use to drain Brussels sprouts?

An advent colander!

===

What's the most popular Christmas wine?

"I don't like Brussels sprouts!"

My Christmas cake has gone missing.

I've reported it as Stollen.

Last year I'd planned to cook my girlfriend a nice Christmas turkey with a herb stuffing...

... but I just couldn't find the thyme.

It was Christmas Eve in a supermarket and a woman was anxiously picking over the last few remaining turkeys in the hope of finding a large one.

In desperation she called over a shop assistant and said, "Excuse me. Do these turkeys get any bigger?"

"No" he replied, "They're all dead."

Which country do the best Christmas chefs come from?

Turkey!

What did the strawberry say to the lemon?

"'Tis the season to be jelly!"

What did the gingerbread man put on his bed?

A cookie sheet!

The boys asked, "Mom, can I have a dog for Christmas?"

She replied, "No, you can have turkey like everyone else!"

What did the packet of Walker's say to the packet of Skips?

Merry Crisp-mass!

What do you get if you deep fry Santa Claus?

Crisp Kringle!

Where did Father Christmas get his fridge?

Comet!

What do snowmen eat for breakfast?

A bowl of snowflakes.

What do snowmen eat for breakfast?

Frosties!

What's Father Christmas' favourite drink?

Beer-d!

What do vampires put on their turkey at Christmas ?

Grave-y

What did the snowman order at McDonald's?

An Iceberg-er!

What does Santa call reindeer that don't work?

Dinner.

We had grandma for Christmas dinner.

Really?

We had turkey.

===

What is a snowman's favorite Drink?

Ice Tea!

===

What kind of cakes do snowmen like?

Iced buns!

===

Who beats his chest and swings from Christmas cake to Christmas cake?

Tarzipan !

===

'ELF AND SAFETY

Santa went to the doctor with a problem:

"What seems to be the problem?" asks the doctor.

"Well, it's very embarassing but I seem to have a mince pie stuck up my bottom!" answered Santa.

The doctor replied, "Don't worry, you're in luck because I've got just the cream for that!"

What do you give a reindeer with an upset tummy?

Elk-a-seltzer!

What do you get if you eat Christmas decorations?

Tinsilitis!

Did you know that Santa's not allowed to go down chimneys this year?

It was declared unsafe by the 'Elf and Safety Commission.

Who looks after Father Christmas when he is sick?

The National 'Elf Service.

What does Santa suffer from if he gets stuck in a chimney?

Claus-trophobia!

Why did Santa call the Mind helpline?

He was worried about his mental elf.

Why did the gingerbread man go to the doctor?

Because he was feeling crummy!

Doctor, doctor, I keep thinking I'm a Christmas bell.

Take these pills and if they don't work, give me a ring.

Why did Santa's helper see the doctor?

Because he had a low "elf" esteem!

What does a Snowman take when he gets stressed?

A chill pill!

LEFT OVERS

What do you call an exploding Christmas tree?
A Tannen-Bomb!

Where do the Irishman keep his Christmas tree?
Between his Christmas two and Christmas four!

Why are Christmas trees like bad knitters?
They both drop their needles!

Which elf was the best singer?
Elf-is Presley.

Why did the elf push his bed into the fireplace?
Because he wanted to sleep like a log!

Where do elves go to dance?
Christmas Balls!

How many letters are in the alphabet at Christmas?

Twenty-four. There's No-EL!

How did Scrooge with the football game?

The ghost of christmas passed!

What comes at the end of Christmas Day?

The letter "Y!"

What do you call a bunch of chess players bragging about their games in a hotel lobby?

Chess nuts boasting in an open foyer!

What do you call a letter sent up the chimney on Christmas Eve ?

Black mail!

What's the slogan for the Eskimo lottery?

You've got to be Inuit to win you it!

What's brown, smelly and sounds like a church bell?

Dung!

What is a librarian's favourite Christmas carol?

Silent Night.

Did you hear about the cracker's Christmas party?

It was a bang!

_____

Why did Jimmy's grades drop after Christmas?

Because everything was marked down!

_____

Why is Christmas a stressful time for toys?

They're all wound up.

_____

What do you need to celebrate Christmas Day on Mount Everest?

Santa's little Sherpa!

_____

What athlete is warmest in winter?

A long jumper!

_____

What happened to the man who stole an Advent Calendar?

He got 25 days!

_____

Why is it always cold at Christmas?

Besauce it's in Decem-brrrrrrr!

_____

Why is it difficult to keep a secret at the North Pole?

Because your teeth chatter!

_____

Merry
Christmas